DATA CONNECTIONS IDEAS

DATA CONNECTIONS IDEAS

NEW ASSETS OF KNOWLEDGE ZENITH ERA

MANOJ SONAWANE

BLISS Services

Contents

1

Preface

The most effective way to convey your idea is still a book. Even those who had technological breakthroughs want to present their idea in the form of a book and thereby bring it to the masses. I have read the story of Elon Musk who built the first prototype of his rocket by reading a book. What type of content you want to consume and what type of problem it will solve for you is completely based on your need or interest. You can build anything by using a book as a tool including your business empire.

We are all on the journey of life and on the timeline of the universe. I can spot my place based on my knowledge, and age. There are many people who are ahead of me in this journey in terms of both knowledge, and age, but there are also many who still need help and this book may guide them and can quench their thirst for growth.

Entrepreneurs build organisations in terms of both

business growth and revenue, but most of them forget that they also need a strong mindset to sustain that business. That's why the first part of this book will help you to create a growth mindset, and then we will move to the second part to build the business in a step-by-step process.

Your social literacy is the key to build a successful organization because your product's position in the market is always based on the social environment. Thus, you need to understand the social system before you enter the business, and hence we have added two chapters on social literacy at the end of this book.

There is a difference between process and practice. The content based on practice is more impactful than the process. Most of the processes are based on theory and hypothetical in nature while practices are real and based on life experiences. We have tried to write this book based on the practices and less of processes (technical stuff).

We change ourselves from time to time and that requires new learning and we approach it through our intuition which changes the course of our lives. This book may help you to put you on the right trajectory and bring the changes you're looking for.

I wish all the best and a big thank you to you and conclude my author note here.

Always stay blessed!

Manoj Sonawane
We change lives through books

2
—

Vote of thanks

A big thank you to my mentors Dr. Sandeep Dongre, Avinash Anand Singh, Praveen Wadalkar, and Amol Karale who shaped my life through their teachings.

I am indebted to my friend Ananda Hajare who helped me to add many diagrams and figures in this book and provided time-to-time support to edit it. He was a great help to me in drawing the figure of data, connections ideas triangle which is featured on the cover page of this book and brought the visual presence of the book idea. I am really very grateful for all your support.

Thank you to my sister Anita Shirsath and brother-in-law Sunil Shirsath who provided me a place to write this book at their home and encouraged me to take many big steps in life.

3

Introduction

It has been found that humankind has developed not only because of their intelligence but also because of their ability to make connections with each other and transfer bits of data across the globe. Earlier data was in the form of knowledge of an individual or a group of people and they were transmitting it by crossing seas, mountains, and forests. This audacious act helped them to exchange ideas or find new paths for a better life of the new generation. They constantly explored new connections for this purpose. Such a network of connections has made humankind more powerful than their animal counterparts who remain separated from each other throughout their lives.

The connection power is applicable everywhere, for example, highly organized and well-connected political party always wins an election and forms a government. The individual who has more connections earns more money. A company that connects their employees for a cause accomplishes more.

Your growth secret lies here. Use this power to harness success in your life. Find your right connections and expand it for more power.

Today we are living in such a golden age where social media is connecting us with each other and paving a way for networking with like-minded people. An individual is getting this connection power in her hand. Use this newfound power for your success.

In this book, we will use words such as connect, connections, values, and causes as platforms or bridges to bond you with the people or surroundings. Now, let's learn below how data, connections, and ideas work for an individual in today's economy.

Data, Connections, and Ideas

The advent of technology has shifted economic power into the hand of common men who have specific knowledge and skill. When we compared it with the earlier generation, we found that a handful of a few had access to data and connections part and was utilizing the local talent (or ideas given by them) to create wealth. Now an individual has direct access to data, connections, and ideas and can use this triangle to generate unlimited wealth and success in their life.

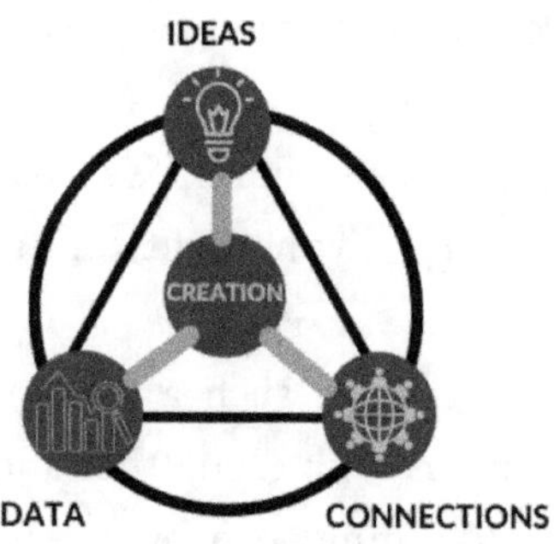

Figure 1. Universe of Creation

Let's consider, you have specific data and built connections with that data group and they need your skill or knowledge to solve their problems. For example, your work is to design websites, and have achieved expertise in website development. You connect with the data group (niche) who needs your expertise. Your knowledge (or ideas) is important for them to build or develop the website. You reach them (connect) through Facebook, LinkedIn, YouTube, Instagram, or Twitter by projecting yourself as a website development expert. Here, you had access to this triangle that is data, connections, and ideas. This triangle becomes the point of creation for you. You, as an individual decide the revenue and the total number of clients to work with. You sell your core expertise. It works like an asset for you and brings incessant wealth. It gives power in the hand of an individual. It's a new asset of the knowledge zenith era.

The most precious thing in your life is time and you can't trade it for something you don't like which may be your current job. Delay in your actions robs the opportunity from you. Remember time is running a race with all of us. Create a system where you can generate wealth. You can get it by going deep into your system. This book will give you real-life examples and frameworks to build your own wealth creation triangle (system). In fact, anyone can build this system, including your plumber or electrician. They just need to know how to do it and build a strong mindset along the way because a strong mindset plays a major role in our success. As Tony Robbins said, success in business has more to do with psychology than skills, experience, or any other single trait. He also shared in one of his tweets that "business success is 80% psychology and 20% mechanics". Thus, build your business on a strong mindset. That's why we have divided this book into two parts, Mindset and Business. This combination works like magic for anyone. Let's explore it in detail.

4

My Story

****

"It's like everyone tells a story about themselves inside their own head. Always. All the time. That story makes you what you are. We build ourselves out of that story."
- Patrick Rothfuss

Before we embark upon the main content of this book, let me share my story with you, and it needs to be added here to take you from mindset to business journey. My parents were farmers, but the strain of producing farm products on shrinking land and unpredictable monsoon, forced them to leave their ancestral village in Jalgaon, Maharashtra, India (this region is also known as Khandesh) and they had to move to a city like Mumbai. Both, my mother and father, started their life by working as labourers in Mumbai. First, my father migrated to this city in the year 1965 through

8

a reference of a fellow villager, named Babu Mukadam (Mukadam means the head of the labourer). Mukadam used to visit our ancestral village frequently in search of labourers. On one of such visits, he approached my father and offered him a job in Mumbai. He promised my father a steady income if he will work as a labourer in this city of dreams. My father liked Mukadam's offer and decided to migrate to Mumbai.

He came to this city and started working as a labourer in a stone quarry in the Ghatkopar suburb (In Marathi, Ghat means hill and Kopar means corner and the name Ghatkopar literally translates into hill corner). Within a year, he called up my mother to Mumbai. Like any other labourer of that time, they were living in a handmade makeshift home near their workplace. In those days, it was common for women to work with their husbands in the farms in villages. When she came to Mumbai, she continued the same by working as a labourer in a stone quarry and was supporting my father in the earning. Now both were working as labourer in the stone quarry. My father's main job was to fill or empty the truck containing the dust of crushed stone and my mother's job was to collect stones in a pot and pour them into the stone-crushing machine.

As promised by Mukadam, they were getting continuous work in Mumbai. My father was sending some income to my grandparents who lived in the village. Now the basic needs were being met from this income. But we were still in poverty.

Later, my father upgraded himself to only one skill in his life that was driving and he learned it from another truck driver who was working in the stone quarry area. This skill helped him to earn some extra money. He saw this opportunity through the lens of his surroundings.

Now, observe here, my mother knew farm work and she continued to work as a labourer in a stone quarry. My father was first a farm labourer, then worked as a labourer in a stone quarry, and later on, learned driving skills and was a truck driver rest of his life. They were seeing the opportunity through the lens of their surroundings. Their income, belief, behaviour, and habit had come to them through their surroundings. My parents might have been different persons if their surroundings had been different, as we are an average of our surroundings. We will discuss it in more detail in chapter number seven of this book.

My father's life lasted like this nearly for two decades in this city. He died at the age of 41. Can you imagine the situation of a family without a father? My mother, uneducated and was a labourer with five children to feed. But she decided to overcome this crisis. When there is a crisis in the family, women are often more powerful than men to handle it. She took the charge and within a decade she completely turned around things from poverty to financial stability. She encouraged me to pursue higher education and imprinted her dream life on me. She stepped out of her circle and formed new beliefs through her dreams.

My Educational Journey

I remember my mother and I left home early in the morning on the day of my admission in school. I was walking with her, unaware of my destination. About ten minutes later, we reached near one of the buildings. I saw some kids playing on the ground there. They were playing some game and singing this song "fire in the jungle, run, run, run! fire in the jungle, run, run, run!". I was curious to know this game, but my mother didn't allow me to stand and watch it. Next, we entered the building where she was enquiring about the principal's office.

We reached and waited outside the principal's office for our turn to discuss about my admission. My mother seemed anxious. She must have been thinking about my admission in the school. We were allowed to enter and meet the principal after half an hour. He offered us seats. My mother started the conversation and requested for my admission in school, but her dream was shattered when she received a reply from the principal that "admission are full in our school".

She requested the principal to do something and said "My son's academic year will be wasted if he does not get admission and there is hardly any school in this area except this one".

But he refused to do anything. We left his cabin without any hope. As we walked down a corridor, she suddenly said, "Let's meet Aaji (Grandma)." Aaji named as Kerubai Bhosle was the mother of Karuna, a neighbour, and a friend of my mother. She used to work as a support staff in that school.

Aaji soon came to meet us there in the corridor area. She was our last hope. My mother told her everything. Aaji asked her, "Why are you insisting on admission in the Marathi medium section of this school although the education is the same in both Hindi and Marathi mediums? She further said

"I have been working as support staff in the Hindi medium section and as far as I know, seats are readily available in this section". Let's meet the Hindi medium section principal".

She also suggested us that I could switch from Hindi to Marathi medium section next year if I wanted to. Though my mother tongue is Marathi, my mother agreed to her suggestion and was happy about me not having to lose an academic year. She got me admitted to the Hindi medium section of the municipal school and that is how my education journey started.

I initially faced a language barrier but soon adapted to the new language. Next year, seeing my progress, my mother did not change my section. I completed my Secondary School Certificate (SSC) or Grade 10 from Hindi medium school.

After passing school, I took admission in college and enrolled in the science stream. The language of instruction in the college was English. I remember my first day in college. It was a feeling similar to what I had when I was in Grade 1 after being admitted to the Hindi medium section where "a six-year-old boy who had never heard Hindi words and was clueless about that language".

The students from English-medium schools had an advantage compared to vernacular-medium students like me. They were asking the questions and discussing problems with the facilitator in English. I made up my mind and decided that by the time I will complete my Higher Secondary Certificate (10+2), I would be fluent in English.

However, once you decide to improve on something you actually have to resolve various questions around that problem. I was asking questions like "How to learn English?"; "How to be fluent in English?" and "What can be done to have command over the English language?"

In response to that, I got answers on the lines of 'read English newspapers', 'watch English movies and news channels', 'always talk in English with your friends', etc. I followed it consistently. It worked for me. By the time I passed out Higher Secondary Certificate, I was speaking in English and had command over this language. I overcame the language barrier second time in my life.

English helped me to complete my education and I passed the degrees like B.Sc., M.Sc., and M.L.I.Sc. (Master of Library and Information Science). This language is a precious asset to me to this day.

Reason to Earn Extra Income Sources

After completing my education, I got a job. Soon, I realised that my income through a job was not sufficient enough to buy a home in Mumbai. In my spare time, I was investing my savings in real estate in the suburbs near Mumbai, where prices were within my reach. My income skyrocketed through these sources and it helped me to buy house in Mumbai. I cracked my first crore. I stepped out of my circle and started thinking big. I bought two flats within a few years of doing this, for me and for my mother. In 1965, she was living in a makeshift house, today she lives in an apartment that she can call home. Each of her children has settled down in Mumbai and is living a happier life as compared to first-generation migrant parents.

After analysing my parents and my life, I found that we are an average of our surroundings. We have to break this ceiling (surroundings) periodically and have to come out of our bubble by learning or hanging out with the people who are ahead in the journey of our work. It is the only way for limitless growth and be unstoppable throughout life.

In this book, you'll be introduced to the various tools to help you to break the limiting beliefs and then we will work on a master plan to build the business around your passion. This is like checking your computer's pre-requisite before you install any new software and in the same way breaking of limiting beliefs is a pre-requisite before you start a business or become an entrepreneur. We'll work on these pre-requisite tools before we move to the business part of this book. Build an empire on a solid foundation. In the business part, we will mainly discuss the following wealth creation triangle:

1. First, know the insight of your customer (data).
2. Second, reach out to them by using social media platforms or emails or any other prevalent means of the time and build the network of your tribe (connections).
3. Third, create a product or service that will solve the problem of your tribe (Ideas).

This triangle- your customer insight (data), reaching out to your tribe (connections), and solving their problems by creating products or services (ideas) works like an instant currency as money flows into your bank account through an online marketing campaign.

Learn and absorb the information of this book very carefully. See the flowchart below. We will go step by step and will break each iceberg at a time. In the first part, we will build a limitless mindset, and then in the second part, we will construct a wealth creation triangle. Let's start it from the base.

Know your life's purpose and have goals

Erase your wrong beliefs

Use NLP to reprogram your brain wiring

Create opportunities for lasting growth

Use books to sharpen the lens of your mind

Change the limiting surroundings

Build the data, connections and ideas triangle

Apply Metcalfe's law of economic power

Earn your first crore

Speak to connect

Know your niche

Know the winning traits of a millionaire

School education system

Keep an eye on the Government's policy

Conclusions

Figure 2. Flow of learning

5

Passion and Goal Oriented Life

****

"Your purpose in life is to find your purpose and give your life whole heart and soul to it."

- Buddha

The first tool to form a limitless mindset is to know your life's purpose and have goals. Let us begin this chapter with these questions: "Why didn't my father overcome poverty?" "Why did he die so early?" "Why didn't my mother turn her life around when my father was alive?" "What made her to accomplish everything when she became the decision-maker?"

The answer to the above questions is that every human being needs goals to live a life. It doesn't matter how small or big your goals are, you must have one, whether short-term or long-term. Even a small goal like teaching the English language to rural children in India can enrich you and will make your life worth to live.

My father was in poverty and broke at the end of his life. He died at the age of 41. All these are signs of goal-less life or he may not be aware of life sutras for living. Here is a mantra for life: Have a goal! Have a goal! Have a goal!

It was natural for my mother to take care of her children, but her life became more goal-oriented when she started to dream big for her children. Not only she took complete charge of her family, but also set the goal of her dream life and accomplished it. It was this goal-oriented mindset that helped my mother to overcome poverty. She must be holding all these life-enhancing goals in her mind continuously. Poverty is nothing but a by-product of a goal-less or aimless life.

Here is the complete cycle of goal

Set the goal → Learn the art of achieving it → End it with the art of fulfilment →Set the next goal.

Figure 3. Goal Cycle

For the happiest possible life, keep repeating the above cycle for each and every goal, till the time you die. The goal is a fuel that helps you move forward in life. The art of achieving goals sets the life path whereas acknowledging it with happiness helps you to live a fulfilled life.

Take a moment and check out whether you are missing any link from the above-mentioned goal cycle.

Let me tell you the truth, only happy and successful people follow this cycle knowingly or unknowingly. This cycle is like litmus to check both success and fulfilment part of our life. Setting a goal and achieving it is a success and acknowledging it with a mark of happiness is fulfilment. But many people miss the fulfilment part.

How the Art of Fulfilment Part Works

You live a happy and fulfilled life when you help others. You share your success with family, friends, and those who are in need of it. You help them to grow in the area of your success. The truth is that you grow more by helping others. Being a helping hand marks your life with real happiness that lasts longer than any other footprint in the world. Help others with your "success blueprint". Many miss out the art of fulfilment part by keeping their success or success blueprint with them as a secret and they die wondering why they weren't happy, fulfilled, or content at the end of their life. Successful people are not always the happiest people if they failed to end their success with the art of fulfilment.

Difference between Passion, Success, Goals and Purpose

People are always confused with words like passion, success, goals, and purpose. Here are the differences.

Finding your passion and working on it consistently means finding a purpose in life. You must have a signature of your purpose in your success. Your consistent goals lead you to unlimited success. Goals are like milestones and achieving one goal after another leads you to a higher purpose in life.

It is clear from the above, that words like passion, success, goals, and purpose are interlinked in an individual's life.

How to find passion?

Many people don't know what to do with their lives when their first ten years have gone by. They still don't know after another twenty years. Then, they turn forty, then sixty, and still don't know what to do with their lives. Is there a way to overcome this wandering syndrome? Yes! Just find your passion to overcome this problem. Your passion will free you from unwanted things and helps you to look for things that are important to you. It makes you focus. Remember your passion should be lifeward.

Following are the checkpoints to find your passion

1. You're talking about certain topics or ideas most of the time of the day.
2. You don't feel tired while talking or sharing your life's purpose with anyone.
3. You are an expert when it comes to your area of interest.
4. You feel happy if anything related to your area of interest comes to you.
5. You are improving in your area of interest every day and you can feel and measure it.

Now let's discuss about how to achieve goals

It is well-known that those with goals are successful and those without it are not. Goal setting is an important exercise for everyone, whether you are a teacher, student, business-man, entrepreneur, or doctor. Your goals help you to achieve more in less time. If you have ten things to complete in the next ten days, it means that you have one day for each job. Here each thing is like a goal for you. Prepare a list of your goals and schedule the timeline to accomplish it. You get clarity when you set a schedule for your goals. Don't be in hurry. Achieve your goal one by one.

Preparing your list to do things in advance helps you to

ascertain prominent questions of unresolved issues of those things and can be considered as identified goals. Now, there is a gap between the questions you have and the answers you want to seek. Your mind starts to fill this gap or wants to close this open-loop as soon as possible. Open-loops are un-resolved issues or goals that need to be identified and put in a scheduled program to command your mind to accomplish it.

Suppose you set your goals for the period of one year and it starts on 1st January and ends on 31st December. Then, you have a total of 12 months to accomplish your goals. Prioritise the goal as per your urgency. Remember, you have to finish one goal at a time. If you set 12 goals to complete in 12 months, then you will have one month to complete each goal. Some goals may take a longer time and some may be finished early, but by and large, you are entitled to accomplish them within the specified time limit. Remember that investing your time wisely is the key to your success and goal-setting exercise helps you to manage it appropriately. Below is an example of goals list. This is a list of annual goals. You can also create daily, weekly, monthly, bi-yearly or five yearly goals lists.

Things I must do during this year i.e. not later than 31st December 2023, 12.00 AM.

Sr. No.	Goals

1	Publish the book "Data, Connections, Ideas: New Assets of Knowledge Zenith Era"
2	Watch 30 educational videos related to my subject learning.
3	Finish the writing of 250 pages book and title it as "Script, Edit, Act: 22 Life Lessons from Bollywood Industry".
4	Attend 12 workshops/ webinars related to my work or subject learning.
5	Conduct five workshops on the topic "How to Write a Book and Self publish it".
6	Write down three "Fictional Stories" to sharpen the English writing skill.
7	Launch an e-learning course on "How to Write a Book and Self-publish it".

8	Launch an e-learning course based on my book "Learning 2.0: An Inside Story on Teaching".
9	Create 100 videos on various tools of life.
10	Finish the reading of 52 books.
11	Watch five e-learning courses in my field.
12	Launch "101 Most Influential Books List Templates".

Table 1. Goal List

The goals shape your life's purpose and you attain maximum potential, once you are clear about it. Now, let's move to the next chapter where you'll learn how to erase your wrong or limiting beliefs and fasten the process of achieving success in your life.

6

How to Erase Your Wrong Belief

****

"A belief is not merely an idea that the mind processes; it is an idea that processes the mind."
-Robert Bolton

Let's get to the root of achieving goals. The resources flow to your life through the gate of your mind. Have you ever thought that you had loved a type of dress at some point and when it came to buying, you ended up buying the same type of dress? It happened to you because you had created a unique pattern of that dress in your mind in the form colour, design, fitting, etc. before you actually bought it. This pattern works like a goal in your mind and it directs you towards specifications given by you and you end up buying the same dress.

Goals work in a similar way. You attract the resources based on a pattern (goals specification) created in your mind. Your pattern works like a laser focus which filters out unwanted things. Thus, make your goals intense and clear. You can imprint it in your mind every day by writing it in a notebook (goal diary). Let the mind know what you want consistently and it will direct you toward the resources required to accomplish that goal.

How Do You Accomplish Your Goals?

The pattern you have created in your mind acts like a blueprint (your goal) which is supplied to the reticular activation system (RAS), a kind of filter (made up of a bundle of nerves) located near the brainstem that filters out unimportant information and allow the entry of information related to your blueprint only. That's why you ended up buying the dress you decided in your mind (a kind of blueprint supplied to RAS).

Now, what if you hold certain negative or wrong or limiting beliefs in your mind and are continuously supplying it to your RAS system? It will impact you in that area. Take the example of a student; if she has negative beliefs about any subject, then it affects her on that subject. She will have to change or erase her negative beliefs about it.

How to Erase Negative Belief

Here is the system to erase the negative belief or change

your approach towards that subject. Study the following belief system quadrant.

Potential (2)

If the approach is negative in the learning of a subject, then use the affirmation like "I love the subject___ ___(write the subject name here)" which helps you to be resourceful in that particular subject.

Action (3)

State of resourcefulness opens up the door of action as the person sees that subject in a positive way.

Belief (1)

A person is either positive or negative for any approach including the learning of an academic subject (+ -)

Results (4)

You score good marks in that subject due to resourcefulness and actions.

Figure 4. Belief System Quadrant

It's clear from above, that our belief is either negative or positive towards anything including the subject we want to learn. In the case of a student, she has to list all the subjects. Now, from the list, tick the subject in which she always scores low marks. It indicates that she has certain negativity or has been closed for that subject for quite some time. Thus, she has to open up in it to score good marks by changing her belief from a negative to a positive one.

The next step is to create a positive affirmation for that

subject and say that affirmation consistently which sends a message to the RAS system which in turn considers it important for her.

A positive affirmation opens up the resourceful state in her mind for that subject and draws her attention to the things related or important to it.

As the result, she changed her belief by applying the above system which helps her to score good marks in that particular subject.

You can apply the above system to change your belief for anything. List out all the concerned areas that hold you back. Remember it is just a belief. You need to change it if it is holding you back, for example, take the most common negative belief of most people, such as "I'm not a good public speaker". Apply the above belief system (quadrant) and use a positive affirmation such as "I am an excellent public speaker". This will help you to be an excellent public speaker in a real sense. Remember, here you are activating your RAS system that filters out unwanted things and flows resources related to public speaking such as good books on communications, connecting you with a great public speaker or mentor, etc. All of these things help you to become an excellent public speaker.

In the next chapter, we will deep clean any negative beliefs by using the NLP (Neuro-Linguistic Programming) system.

7

NLP: A Tool to Achieve Your Goal Fast

****

"Change the way you look at things and the things you look at changes."
- Wayne W. Dyer

Let's get deep into this system again and find out how to clean up the negativity and set the goal of achieving extraordinary results in any concerned area. We will take the example of a student who feels negative about a subject like mathematics and can be considered as a concerned subject area. This deep-level clean-up system or reinstalling new belief is called as Neuro-Linguistic Programming (NLP) and is a very effective system to erase any negative belief (limiting software) from your mind completely. It can be applied to any limiting belief of your life that holds you back.

Neuro-Linguistic Programming (NLP)

Neuro-Linguistic Programming or NLP is a new term for success. It is widely used by counsellors, consultants, coaches, managers, engineers, athletes, entrepreneurs, executives, parents, etc. It is a technique where a person can change his/her behaviour or old negative conditioning and can achieve great results in anything. As mentioned above, we'll take the example of a student who feels negative about a subject like mathematics and will use the NLP system to break this negative belief (pattern). Let's say her limiting belief is "I am not good in mathematics". I have simplified the NLP steps below to erase this limiting belief. The examples used below are for your guiding purpose.

Step 1. Create a new vision of your study goal. Use the sentence in the present tense as our brain perceives everything as now.

Step 2. Create powerful declarations and affirmations that support that new vision.

Step 3. Develop emotional anchors for neural linking.

Step 4. Prepare a portfolio of imprinting material.

Step 5. Maintain a brief daily routine of reconditioning techniques three times a day (after waking up, at midday, and before bed).

All these steps are elaborated below for your reference.

NLP Steps:

-

Step 1 - Vision

1. My total mark in mathematics is 100 out of 100 (or whatever the maximum possible score).

Step 2 – Affirmation

1. I love the subject mathematics.
2. I love to teach or learn mathematics at any time.
3. Mathematics is a scoring subject.
4. I am a genius in mathematics.
5. Everyone is helping me to be an expert in mathematics.

Step 3 - Neural Linking

Linking the solid example for your affirmation is called neural linking. For example, neural linking for the affirmation like "I am a genius in mathematics" is given below:

"I was in complete control while solving the mathematics problem on my classroom board. I received admiration from my friends and teachers. I was admired as "a genius girl in mathematics". This helps you to make that statement true in a real sense. You can take any incidence like this to make the neural linking strong.

Step 4 - Prepare your neural imprinting material

Laminate your vision. Use a vision board where you can paste pictures of your future achievements, like your photo holding the placard of the sentence "My total marks in mathematics is 100 out of 100" and look at this photo thrice daily, in the morning, at midday, and before bedtime.

Step 5 - Neural Reconditioning Process

Do the following thrice a day, in the morning, at midday, and before bedtime. Follow the below steps in sequence.

1. Meditations: Close your eyes and concentrate at the centre of your two eyes. Do not think for at least ten minutes. Calm your mind and meditate.
2. Visualisations: Run a moving picture of your goals or vision in your mind.
3. Affirmation: Write or declare the affirmation. Examples are given above.

It is guaranteed that after 21 days you will feel the change and will subsequently achieve speedy success in the subject mathematics.

Now your mind gives priority to mathematics and diverts your attention to the things important to this subject and helps you to improve in it day by day. Earlier you were ignoring it, due to a hate pattern for it. You have reprogrammed your brain wiring to like the most-hated subject by using the above system. You can use these steps to reprogram the wrong/hate pattern (or limiting beliefs) for anything including a business or relationships.

We are done with the science of achieving goals. Now let's move to the chapter on how to create opportunity.

8

How to Create an Opportunity

"When we leverage, we aggregate and organize existing resources to achieve success."

- Richie Norton

Let's take real-life examples of persons who depended on someone to make things happen for them and waited for a single opportunity for a decade. A few years back I was in Jalgaon, a district in Maharashtra, India. I was in a stay at my maternal uncle's place. During a casual conversation with my uncle, he told me that how people here, have been selling their farms or lands and paying a certain amount to officials of government-aided schools or colleges to get the jobs of a lecturer, teacher, or peon in the institutions. This amount varies as per the posting: 7 to 10 lakhs rupees for a peon; 12 to 15 lakhs for a teacher; and 25 to 30 lakhs for a lecturer (One Lakh=hundred thousand Indian rupees or US$1333). The competition is intense here and these officials award the post to the highest bidder.

If the school or college is not granted by the government, then these trust officials appoint the teachers or lecturers on a temporary basis and exploit them by paying meagre salaries in the range of 5,000 to 12,000 rupees per month. They promise to provide continuous service and pay scale in the future if the institution will get a grant from the government.

There are many examples where people have worked for seven to twelve years on a temporary basis but trust officials rejected their appointments and sold these posts like commodities in a market. My maternal uncle told me about two such incidents. In the first, a teacher who worked for more than seven years in a school but later on they forced him to resign from the post because he was unable to pay the said amount. The trust recruited another candidate who had paid more. The age of this person was 37 when they told him to leave the post. But he has to feed his family and now runs a cycle repairing shop on the road. He is B.A, B.Ed. After hearing his story, I met him in person. But he does not believe that there are more opportunities out there.

In another case, a lecturer who had been working in a college for more than 12 years. After regularising his post from the government, college authorities forced him to resign from his post as he was unable to pay the said amount. The institution wanted to sell his post in an open market. The lecturer tried to file a case against the college officials, but they threatened him to do anything like this. He had been admitted to the hospital after that incident.

From the above two incidents, I was forced to believe that people in smaller towns have limited exposure to opportunities or information as compared to their urban counterparts. It is our responsibility to find a way to bridge this gap so that they will believe that there are more opportunities out there and that there are ways to create it.

How to Create an Opportunity and Get the Early Success?

Assess a skill that you will find easy to adapt. You can figure it out at any age but it is best to know before the child reaches the age of 10. If you're a parent, help your child to recognise his/her skill at an early age. According to studies, a person can become an expert in any skill, once she crosses the threshold of focus 10,000 hours of experience by doing it.

How to do this? Practice the identified skill for at least six hours a day. A person, who does this, reaches 10,000 hours of experience after five years (365 days X 5.5 hours = 2,007.5 hours a year; 2,007.5 X 5 years = 10,037.5 hours). Thus, by the age of 15, she can become an expert in her chosen field.

If you followed the above rule and attained the expertise at an early age, imagine the impact of such skillsets, not only in earning money but also in adding value in that field. People will recognise you based on your expertise, as society remembers people who provide value to them than the people who don't know what to do with his/her life or are aimless.

Certain communities in India are aware of this secret. There is another reason that most of them run family businesses for several generations. Though they hold the business across generations but they pass it on to the next generation successfully. They start to hand over business skills to their children at an early age. They teach them every business move and make things automatic for them. They evolve through various processes concerned to their business. They identify sequences of executing any tasks in their business and make the replicas of it and hand over these replicas to the next generation who in turn work on it repeatedly till the time it becomes automatic for them and they also take it to the next level. Whether they are aware of it or not, but they be at the top of business skills once they cross the focus 10,000 hours of experience in running it.

Use this rule to achieve expertise in anything. Figure out your skill whether you want to build a business, invest in properties, or learn football and drawing skills or anything. Your next step must be to cross the focus 10,000 hours of experience in doing it. Remember, as per research, it is a threshold to attain expertise.

In the above two incidents of the Jalgaon, the institutions might have hinted their intention to them in many ways much earlier. They should have started to create alternate sources/opportunities while working for them. There was enough window period for them to cross the threshold and be powerful before someone pounces on them. They depended on that single opportunity to be provided to them by someone else and in the end, they failed to get it. Thus, assess the skill and become an expert in it. You will stand out differently and would be in demand.

Make sure that you read a lot of books to identify opportunities for you. Let's learn how to read more books in the next chapter.

9

Book- A Tool to Sharpen the Lens of Your Mind

****

"Our life changes in two ways: through the people we meet and the books we read."

- Harvey Mackay

Books play an important role in everyone's life but often we hear from people that they don't have time to read books (and grow rich in the process). Here is a way to read 52 books in 52 weeks (1 Year) and sharpen the lens of your mind by using it as a tool.

How to Read 52 Books in 52 Weeks?

If you're watching television or surfing the internet for two to three hours a day, and if you can reduce this time by an hour a day, then you will have 365 extra hours a year. If you divide that by a forty-hour workweek, you'll see that you have added about nine-and-a-half additional weeks of productivity to your life. That is two additional months every year. Use this additional hour to read books on self-esteem, self-management, motivation, education, and training. It's sure that it will make a profound difference in your life.

If you're not ok with one hour of daily reading, then just keep fifteen minutes aside in a day. In fact, you can read a book a month which amounts to twelve books a year by reading only fifteen minutes every day. Here's how:

The average high school students read 250 words a minute. But we all stop to re-read a sentence from time to time... or pause to think about new ideas. So, it's fair to say that the average reading rate for most adults is 200 words a minute.

There are about 400 words on an average book page, which means the average reader should be able to read it in two minutes. At this rate, you can read seven pages in 15 minutes.

Suppose there are 210 pages in a book. So, by reading 15 minutes (seven pages) a day, you can read this book in 30 days. It may take you more than a month to read longer books, but by and large, if you read 15 minutes a day, you'll be able to finish a book a month.

By the end of the year, you'll have read at least 12 books. By the end of 10 years, that will add up to 120 books! Just think, by setting aside 15 minutes a day, you can easily read

120 books that may help you grow richer in all areas of your life. By doubling your daily reading time to just half an hour, you can read 25 books a year – 250 books in 10 years. Again, if you double your daily reading time to just an hour, you can read 50 books a year – 500 books in 10 years. You can see that reading 52 books in 52 weeks (1 Year) is possible by using the above strategy.

That's why one should not be sympathetic to people who say that they don't have the time to read the book and grow rich. That's nonsense. They have the time. They're just choosing to use their time doing something they value more than reading.

It's sure that reading habits will sharpen the lens of your mind, which will help you to scan more opportunities around you. Use books as a tool to achieve greater success in your life.

In the next chapter, we will learn about why and when to upgrade our limiting surroundings.

10

Change the Limiting Surroundings

"If you don't get out of the box you've been raised in, you won't understand how much bigger the world is."
- Angelina Jolie

In the early 90s in Mumbai, a teenage boy dreams of being a bad boy as he thinks that it's the only way to make a mark in society. Every evening, he goes out with bad company. He imitates their bad language, behavior, and gestures and he enjoys this life. His role model is an elderly boy of the group and he dreams to be like him one day.

One evening, that elderly boy took him and one of his friends out, for some work. Both of them were unaware of that elderly boy's plan, but they enjoyed his company, and they thought that they got the chance to make a mark now. It was like blindfolded faith on him. He takes them to an old paper mart shop and on reaching there, that elderly boy took out his knife. He goes near the shop owner and threatens him with his knife for the money. The shop owner immediately locks his drawer (containing money in it) and throws the key toward his wife and shouts loudly for help. The moment he shouts, that elderly boy runs out fast and both the boys follow him and while running, he hands over his knife to one of the boys and runs away from the spot quickly. This shop was located near the traffic signal and it so happened that one of the cops had been passing through that signal on his bicycle that time and he heard the commotion. He stopped and threw his bicycle and ran towards both the boys. They were running as fast as possible, but the cop caught hold of one of the boys within a few minutes. Another boy surrendered to the cop, after finding his friend had been caught by the cop. The cop was beating both boys mercilessly. But he let off the boys after finding them underage and just noted their names and age in his diary and asked the name of that elderly boy who was spoiling them and left the spot.

The above story is a true story and the boy who surrendered to the cop is the author himself and the only difference is that the he considers great people as his role model today. The above incident was a major turning point in my life and it transformed me completely. Since that day, I never saw that elderly boy and changed my friend circle.

I never thought to change this surrounding prior to this incident. I am really grateful to the cop who beat us mercilessly that day. But he let us go without registering a complaint against us. We had a taste of the bad world first time in our life.

During the late 80's and early 90's, many teenage boys in Mumbai were fascinated to the 'Tapori' lifestyle. 'Tapori' literally translates into rowdy in English and they love to speak in their unique style called as 'Tapori' language. It may be because of the influence of Bollywood movies of that time which were glorifying the hero as a 'Tapori' and both the boys wanted to imitate this rowdy living in a real life.

Understand here, we see the world through the lens of our surroundings. It limits us and breaks our broad views of life. Yes, it's true, to bring a major change in our life, we need to change our surroundings periodically as it helps us to break the limiting beliefs governed in our group of people.

When to Change Your Limiting Surroundings?

When you feel, you are stuck and not growing in life, then, look around, and observe your surroundings and you will find that your income, belief, and behavior, is an average of your five friends. As mentioned in the introductory chapter, one has to break this ceiling and come out of this bubble by hanging out with the people who are ahead in a journey or in the field of your work. Always look for limitless growth. Change the limiting surroundings. Your surroundings matter a lot in your growth.

Now, we are done with the mindset part of this book and I want to congratulate you on completing it. Let's move to the next part, as you have built the mental foundation by using the insights from chapters one to seven and now you are ready for both business and financial growth.

11

Data, Connections and Your Ideas!

"A business is simply an idea to make other people's lives better."

- Richard Branson

If we compare the mindset part with the business skills, 80% would be given to mindset and 20% to skills. That's why we emphasize the first part of this book on building a mindset, as it creates a solid mental foundation to do anything. Let's discuss the business and entrepreneurship part now.

Why to Invest in Self Education and Skill?

Before we discuss business and entrepreneurship let me

tell you the true story of one of my colleagues. She had been working for a company for many years and was dependent on a job for income. She got too comfortable and was not doing anything concrete that would set her free from the energy and time she was putting in her work which was more repetitive. One day, the company announced that they will review the work profile and compensation of each employee. They found the compensation too high for her work profile and asked her to leave the company.

New industries are coming up. Old ones are falling. Those who are not fit for the new industries skillsets would be outdated. Invest your time and money in developing new skills or getting a new education. Learning new skills and combining them with existing skills creates many new ideas and they also serve a fuel for your workplace growth. You'll end up being nowhere by just working for someone else in the 21st century. Escape from this default life template where you have been scripted as a wilful servitude and replace it with self-endorsed work which needs massive action. As Thomas Henry Huxley said, "The great end of life is not knowledge but action". Take it now! Emphasize more on self-education and self-endorsed work.

Investing in self-education will help you to find your passion which you can turn into an idea and then into a product or service. Focus on one idea at a time. Consider it as a potential business and act like an entrepreneur.

How to Stretch Your Passion into an Idea?

Every task, like sports or a job has a set of rules, and one needs a set of skills to complete it. We will get bored if the rules for completing a task are too basic or relative to our skillsets. On the other hand, if, we assign ourselves a task that is too difficult, we won't have the skill to complete it and will almost certainly give up and feel frustrated. The ideal is to find a middle path, something aligned with our abilities but a bit of a stretch, so we experience it as a challenge. It's like adding a little something extra that gets you out of your comfort zone. For example, if I am fond of reading, then the next level would be writing my own book and publishing it and selling it as a product.

Work on pattern, identity and pain area (PIP System) before you create a product or service based on your ideas:

1. Create your pattern
2. Create your identity
3. Know the pain area of your customer

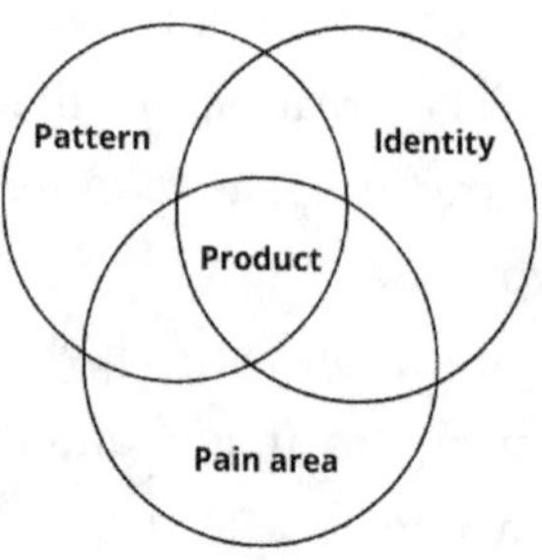

Figure 5.PIP System

1) Create Your Pattern:

Your passion helps you to set your pattern and people recognise you on the basis of your pattern. Here, people see a pattern first before knowing your passion. Don't change the pattern constantly. Be consistent and stick to one area. It helps you to build your connections and attracts the right people to your tribe. Like, I set it around books, reading, writing, and teaching.

2) Create Your Identity

After creating the pattern, create your identity. Your identity should be the evolution of your pattern. Remember that your designation in an organisation is like a temporary mask. The mask may fall at any of the time. It doesn't matter how many jobs you change or change your positions or retire. The mask is going to fall and such a moment will be like an identity crisis for you. When I changed my last organization, the first thing I did is to work on my identity and decided to make it separate from my position or post. My Identity is now author, storyteller, mentor, and education strategist. It is far safe to create your identity rather than maintaining your position in an organisation. It will give you a reason to create your own product and serve to your tribe. Strengthen your personal brand by building your pattern and identity and then create a product because it gives people reason to believe in you and they buy a product from you.

2) Know the Pain Area of Your Customer

It's a story from my life. Somewhere in the late 1980s, I

was standing outside a wine shop, selling cooked chickpeas to labourers who were entering inside that wine shop. Within an hour, I sold out all my cooked chickpeas. They were buying it from me to reduce the bitter taste of the alcoholic drink. At that time, I was nine years old. My first investment was five rupees. The total profit created out of it was around forty rupees. I wanted to do it again, but my mother didn't allow me to do it out of fear of drunkard surroundings.

After many years, I realised that by selling cooked chickpeas to labourers outside that wine shop was the right market. The profit generated from that market was huge compared to the investment. The bitter taste of alcoholic drinks was their pain and they wanted to reduce it by eating cooked chickpeas. The lesson here is, if you want to generate a huge profit in any market, then you just need to find a pain area of that market.

How to Build a Business Around Your Passion or Become an Entrepreneur?

As a Library and Information Science (LIS) professional, it was natural for me to embark on a journey of authorship and create a book as a product and sell it worldwide via Amazon and email. As mentioned earlier, solve the problem of people (pain area) through your product or service. Before writing the book, I was analysing the topics for my first book and zeroed on one of the common problems (or pain areas) of teachers that are primarily related to learning and teaching methods, and I found solutions for them in my book 'Learning 2.0: An Inside Story on Teaching'. This time I found the chickpeas in the form of a book. Within a few months of its release, the book became the #Amazon bestseller in the "Educational Philosophy" category. This book has also been featured in the Free Press Journal newspaper. All of this gave me and my book widespread publicity.

First, I demolished my old limiting mindset by using the tools mentioned in the first part of this book and then created a product based on my passion. It helped me to get rid of my mediocrity. Remember, there is a problem with mediocrity. If the work of a person is mediocre, then he/she will be left severely alone. Opposite of that, if he/she comes out of mediocrity and creates a masterpiece, then the reward would be widespread recognition and acknowledgment.

Now let's get to the point, of how I started making money from my book and how a product like this is helping me generate consistent passive income and wealth.

I targeted my first niche, the schools. It is easy to market your product or service once you are clear about your niche.

Then the next question arises, "How to target your niche and get passive income?" Let's analyse it by using the wealth creation triangle.

How to Use the Data, Connections, and Ideas Triangle to Generate Wealth?

Emails:

Find the list of schools in India on the internet. Research on various schools and their boards. After analysing, we observed that two major boards are providing quality infrastructure for the education in India and they are ICSE and

CBSE board schools. They also have good budgets for educational products and services. I created a database of such schools with their email addresses.

During our pre-sale research, we found that ICSE and CBSE board schools are located all over India and they are more than 36,000 in number. Now one needs to set revenue targets. Let us look at it below:

According to the analysis, 10% of the 36,000 schools are expected to purchase such products, bringing the total number of buyers to 3,600.

Now let's move to price analysis. We had fixed a transaction cost of 300 rupees for each book. Here is a profit breakup: 35% of it goes to Amazon as we sell it on Amazon e-commerce platforms across India (it includes shipping and handling fees) and that amount is 105 rupees. The cost of printing is around 85 rupees. That is a total of 185 rupees. Thus, the total profit from per book sale is 300 – 185= 115 rupees. The revenue generated from 3600 buyers is 3600 x 115 = 4,14000 rupees.

Schools are one niche among academic institutions. If we go further, we may have colleges and universities to sell such products. If we consider the world as a marketplace, then remember you just need one right product to sell it all over the world. It helps you to create lifetime wealth. The school email list would be a goldmine for you. You can sell more educational products or services related to the schools in the future.

Now analyse the above part in terms of the wealth creation triangle, here:

1. Schools are your niche - ICSE and CBSE schools (data)
2. List of emails to reach out to schools (connections)
3. The book is your product (idea).

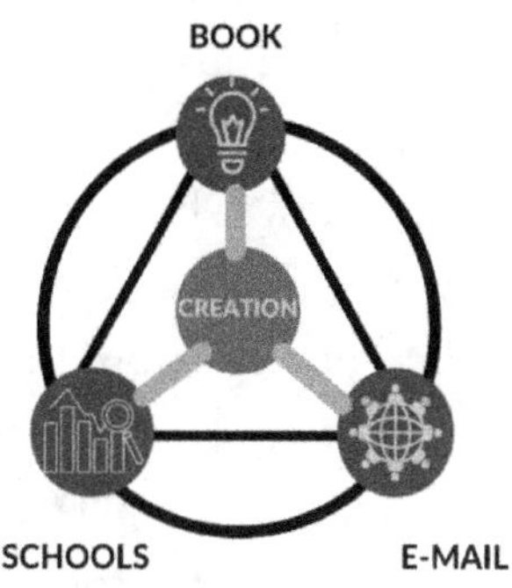

Figure 6. The Wealth Creation Triangle of Book, Schools, and Email

Mapping your business based on this triangle gives you great power. Your data, connections, and idea may be different but it forms the same logic or base. It impacts the business if you miss any of it. Each angle plays an important role and supports each other in a wealth creation triangle here. Now let's take the example of social media and analyse this triangle again.

Social Media:

You need to build your authority on social media and earn the right (ETR) before you sell any product or service on such platforms. First, nurture your audiences through your content. For example, if I am a gym instructor, then I will give health and fitness-related content to my audiences. You can also build the database of your niche through a lead magnet like creating a health or fitness brochure and giving it free to your audiences. It helps you to get the details of your niche like name, email and phone numbers. This also helps you to build your follower base on social media. Once you earn the right by giving value to your audiences, then the next step will be product creation. In this example, you can create different types of products like gym subscriptions, personal training or consultation, or publishing a book on fitness or health. The audience built through this way is called an 'organic audience'.

If you run Facebook Ads or any other social media campaign to attract the buyer for your products or services who are unknown to you, then, such audiences are called 'inorganic audiences'.

We used both types of audiences organic and inorganic to promote the book "Learning 2.0: An Inside Story on Teaching".

Organic- Facebook friend page, Facebook business Page.

Inorganic- School email list, Facebook Ads.

Now analyse the social media part in terms of the wealth creation triangle, here:

1) Social media gives you audience insight (data)

2) You reach out to your audiences by using social media platforms (connection)

3) You sell your product in the form of a book (idea)

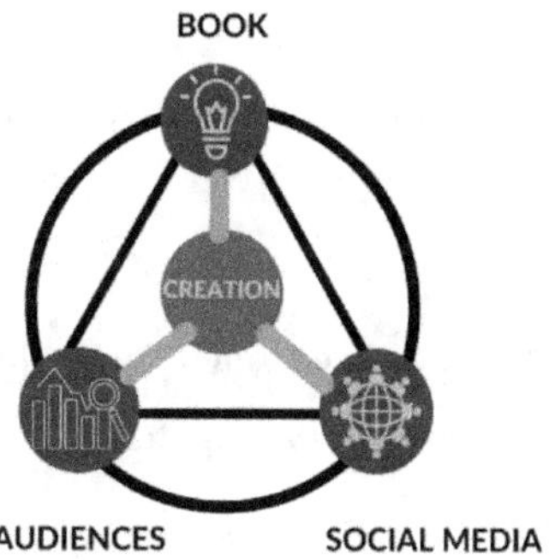

Figure 7. The Wealth Creation Triangle of Book, Audiences, and Social Media

We used both email marketing tools and Facebook ads to attract inorganic buyers. Your copywrite (sale script) or sale drafting plays a crucial role in attracting inorganic buyers. Below are examples of email and Facebook ads drafting for such audiences.

Email draft sent to schools

Subject Headline: Valuable Content for Your Learning Resource Center/Library

*We are happy to share with you that book "Learning 2.0: An Inside Story on Teaching" has reached #1 Amazon Bestseller spot out of top 100 books under the category of **"Educational Philosophy"**.*

This book is mainly written for teaching faculties, students and parents. What you'll get from the book:

1) How to connect with students (or children) using stories (1-minute stories).

2) How to create new content (stories) and use them in learning and teaching methods.

3) Learning Psychology- Learn how to remove the fear of any subject by using NLP (Neuro-Linguistic Programming).

4) Accelerated learning- Learn how to involve students in a self-learning process where teachers (or parents) have to act as mediators and let the students learn and act themselves.

All four parts are based on contemporary methods implemented in the education field in recent times.

Reserve your copy through Amazon as we have limited edition of this book.

Best Regards,

XYZ

We change lives through books

Content for Facebook ads had been different as people open Facebook for entertainment. We need to engage them through a brief story. Following is the actual insight of the Facebook Ads.

Facebook Ads drafting example

Imagine a class where students are excited to hear you; they want to listen to you because you know how to connect with them. The vibes you create bind all of them together and you feel excitement all round.

You can create such excitement in the class through a story. You just need "1- minute" story to connect with the students before you begin a class.

It's like preparing a soil of teaching through a story before you bow the seed of learning. As we are born to interact and express our thoughts, emotions and ideas first in the form of a story. This creates an empathy which in turn connects us with each other.

Learn how to create "1- minute story" and connect with the students by using the insight from the book "Learning 2.0: An Inside Story on Teaching" and supercharge your learning and teaching outcome of a class.

Following are few achievements of this book:

◇ This book has reached #1 Amazon Bestseller Spot under the category of "Educational Philosophy".

◇ It got featured in the Free Press Journal newspaper and received a following review:

"Learning 2.0" by Manoj Sonawane could well be considered an informative dossier for all those who want to acquire knowledge as well as pass it on to others, the book has much wider reach and implications, beyond teacher-pupil domain".

This book is packed with valuable content worth thousands of rupees of training.

Reserve your copy from the link given below as we have a limited edition of this book.

Both Facebook ads and email marketing campaigns yield 10% results if organised as per the above method. Imagine that you have a database of 36,000 leads and are ready to sell other products like this in the future. Even if you have a minimum profit margin of 100 rupees for per transaction, you will earn revenue of 360,000 rupees (10% return rate or 3600 buyers) from your leads with this real-time model.

You can create more products or services based on your book to skyrocket your revenue further. Following are a few examples.

1. Conduct the workshop on how to write a book (based on your book-writing experience)
2. Conduct the webinar or workshop based on the idea of a book (like data, connections, ideas business model)
3. Create an e-learning course based on your book and sell it through webinars/seminars or Facebook ads

A single idea helps you to weave many products around it and takes your expertise to the next level. It all started with the publication of a book. First, it helped you to brand your name on Google and various other social media platforms. Then, you set to be an expert or mentor for others and help them to replicate your business model. You can see how it triggers every time you act on it and it takes you to the next level. You become unstoppable.

Above is the example of creating a book as a product first and then creating many other products or services based on it. It may be different in your case like creating a product (other than the book) mostly around the pain area and then writing a book based on your experience to create your authority. In this case, you may not earn money through your book, but it will help you to build your authority and also brand your business in the marketplace.

Is this Triangle (Data, Connections and Ideas) applicable to Educational Institutions?

Yes, this triangle is not only applicable to an individual like a website development expert discussed in the introduction chapter or in the above model of building a book-based business but also to the educational institutions where they have to gain the insights of parents and students (by collecting data) and based on this understanding management will bond with them through their institutional values (connect). Next, they need to bring continuous innovation in teaching and learning methods to be relevant in the educational space (ideas). Here, all three angles need to be balanced to run the institution effectively.

Thus, business is all about data, connections, and ideas. Take a moment and check if you have missed any angle in your business or think about your own triangle if you are yet to ascertain it.

In the next chapter, we will discuss why your business model should have more than one product/service or sources of incomes to help you build a financial freedom model.

12

Metcalfe's Law of Economic Power

"Opportunities multiply as they are seized."

- Sun Tzu

Find the pain area, and create a product or service out of it. Next, use your first product as a base and create more other products or services around it as it helps you to generate more revenue streams for you. Such a strategy aligns your business with Metcalfe's law of economic power and makes you financially powerful. Let's discuss it below.

Metcalfe's Law of Economic Power.

Metcalfe's law states that the value of a telecommunications network is proportional to the square of the number of connected users of the system. The same law applies to finance as well and can be used to evaluate the economic power of an individual in following way: the economic power of an individual is proportional to the square of the number of businesses or revenue streams created in the system. For example, if an individual holds one business, then her economic power will be one.

1 (individual): 1^2 (business or income sources) = 1:1X1 =1:1

The moment she has two businesses or income sources, her economic power will be 4.

1: 2^2 = 1: 4

You can now figure out, why many of the major business houses hold more than one business or income source at any time. They align with Metcalfe's Law of Economic Power.

1 (TATA): 100^2 (business or income sources) = 1: 10000

Imagine the economic power of an individual, if she holds more than 10 businesses (or income sources). But it is sad that many of the people live a 1:1 life. It is a key law to step into the realm of financial freedom and you should use it in your favour.

Create your first product. Make it successful. You can easily figure out more products out of it. It works like a chain of reaction, where your one action leads to another and helps you to create multiple products or services and you truly apply Metcalfe's Law of Economic Power. Don't wait for the right time. Work on whatever you have. Eventually, you'll find the way while doing it. Take the action.

Where to Start?

Many people always ask questions like, where to start? Here is the answer: it always starts with your passion and one must consider it as the starting point. If possible find a mentor to figure out your passion. Your big dreams will be hollow if you can't find the things you love most and create a product out of it. Never stop to find it. Push for it and keep on pushing until the time you find it. This attitude builds your "idea of life" and takes you forward without much effort and one day it will help you to reach the breakthrough point.

In the next chapter, we will ascertain the amount of money needed for your financial freedom based on your breakthrough idea or product, or service.

13

Key to Financial Freedom: How to Earn Your First Crore

"There is only one success- to be able to spend your life in your own way."

-Christopher Morley

This chapter will help you to figure out the amount of money needed for your financial freedom. We will use the business strategy mentioned in chapter eight, as an example to arrive at your financial freedom figure. Let's say your financial freedom figure is one crore (ten million in Indian rupees or US$ 1,33,870 which is a huge amount in India). Then feed this question to your mind that "How to earn a crore in a year?" Many people will spend a lifetime to earn one crore but they will not figure out how to earn this amount. In fact, you can earn it according to a set plan and set date. It is up to you, how fast you want to earn it. It's like you put 100% energy into your business or work and in return you get 100% money. People who achieve great success in life are people who are willing to do anything to make their dreams come true.

As we have mentioned in the previous chapter and find out the product or service, let's assume that you have a book as a product and one transaction from the sale of a book like "Learning 2.0: An Inside Story On Teaching" creates a profit margin of 115 rupees for you. As per statistics, there is always a 10% return rate for any online marketing such as email, Facebook or SMS reach out if it is done based on the interest of the target audiences. Let's analyse it in the next table:

Serial. No.	Total reach through email, Facebook, SMS	10% realisation (actual buyer)	Average profit per transaction	Total profit created
1	36,000	3,600	115	4,14,000
2	72,000	7,200	115	8,28,000
3	1,44,000	14,400	115	16,56,000
4	2,88,000	28,800	115	33,12,000

| 5 | 5,76,000 | 57,600 | 115 | 66,24,000 |
| 6 | 11,52,000 | 1,15,200 | 115 | 1,32,48,000 |

Table 2. Marketing Plan

As per the above table, you have created a profit of 1,32,48,000. You can subtract the 32 lakhs as overhead or marketing charges. It is clear from the above table, that one needs to reach around 11,52000 leads to achieve the target of one crore rupees in one year to sell a product like a book. Remember, it is easy to reach or generate 11,52000 leads in the world of the internet and social media where one can fetch millions of views for an educational video worldwide.

The same rule applies to training, coaching, or consultation businesses where you can charge a higher cost with less reach out. Here, you only have to reach 100 clients, where each will pay you 1,00,000 rupees and you achieve your target of one crore rupees.

What if you are using this strategy to earn an entire year's salary or package in one month and fulfil your life purpose in the remaining 11 months? Earn more money in less time and use your free time to create more ideas. Your ideas will earn more money for you. It's a slingshot strategy. Follow the deep work philosophy in your spare time by separating yourself from unwanted work and focus on the work that is most important to you. This will help you to create more ideas and in return, you will get more money.

In the next chapter, we will learn high-income skills like storytelling and presentation skills. It will help you to make your business more successful.

14

Speak to Connect

****

"After nourishment, shelter, and companionship, stories are the thing we need most in the world".
-Philip Pullman

Connecting to your audience through your speech/presentation is a learnable skill. The best way to connect with them is to use or tell a story. If we allow two enemy kings to sit together and share their life stories, it is likely that they will end all wars between them because stories create empathy that connects people with each other. Thus, you can use a story as a tool to connect with anyone.

Your story must have three ingredients that are setup, struggle, and success. Struggle forms an important part of these segments. No struggle no story, as we know that human beings love to know the sufferings of others. Developing story-weaving skills would be an additional asset to your business success.

The story mentioned in chapter one has all three ingredients of the above-mentioned structure. The setup: ground, school, principal cabin, corridor, college, etc. The struggle: to gain admission in school and the barrier to speak in Hindi and English language. And success: getting admission in a Hindi medium school, overcoming the language barriers, and completing the education.

How to Present Your Story?

Checklist for your opening presentations:

1. Once your name is announced, walk towards the stage with a little energy.
2. Once on stage and while doing a handshake with the host look into his eyes and say thank you (in other words, you are taking over the stage from the host).
3. Then stand at the centre of the stage by making the steeple hand and pan the audience for three to five seconds (power pause).
4. Always open your speech using these three sentences: 1) I remember, 2) Imagine and 3) Your direct question to the audience, for example, "Have you ever experienced the pain of facing losses in your business?" After that, start your speech on the main content.
5. You can use two more hand poses during a talk: the power pose (use it when high on energy in presenting

any point) and the beggar's hand (use it to evaluate the points).

Checklist for Closing Presentations:

Bring the signature end to your presentation (the signature end means is to bring out the core of your speech and give a message to your audience). Never say the following sentences at the end:

1. I hope you liked my talk/presentation.
2. I hope you enjoyed my session.
3. How many of you liked this speech?

Factors that Connect You with the Audience:

The following three hormones are the main factors that connect you with your audience:

1. Cortisol
2. Dopamine
3. Oxytocin

Cortisol creates attention (when you use the words "I remember", the audience will start to think, what the presenter remembers?).

Dopamine keeps the audience hooked and makes them curious to know what is next. You can release this hormone by providing vivid details of your story, for example, in my personal story in the opening chapters of this book and under the heading of my educational journey, I have put details like early morning time, walking on the road, children's song, etc.

Oxytocin is the hormone that makes your audience emotional and connects heart to heart. They are also called love hormones. In my personal story, the mother's struggle to get her child admitted to school, the child facing language barriers, etc., can be cited to as parts of the struggle of the story, and content like this releases oxytocin hormones.

The same can be applied to a business story where you can use the segments like setup, struggle, and success to structure your business story to connect with your audience. Here your story will be based on your business experience.

As John Haidt said, the "human mind is a story processor, not a logic processor". It is a connecting point between two beings. Create your story bank. Use these stories to connect with your clients or stakeholders. Your story bank will be key to your success. The more stories you have, the more successful you will be. You will also feel more compassionate by using stories in day-to-day life.

In the next chapter, we will discuss about how to leverage social media in your favour and be a celebrity in your micro-niche.

15

Know Your Niche

"Commit to a niche; try to stop being everything to everyone".
-Andrew Davis

In the past, only a handful of traders were controlling the market. It consisted mainly of hoarding goods, manipulating prices artificially, and passing the profits among themselves. A new businessman was an outsider to them.

Now the rules of business have changed. The advent of the internet and technology has given a business command in the hand of the common man. Prices, profits, and partnerships are more transparent today than ever before in history. Technology is helping us to control and track the transaction of each product. The profit is distributed to the end customer. The partnership concepts have been introduced to sell more products online (like a partnership of merchants with e-commerce giant Amazon). You just need a single product to scale up your business on such a platform and it is possible to sell tons of copies of it if you consider the whole world as a marketplace and the internet as a tool to reach out to them.

Trainers, coaches, and consultants are making a fortune by using social media platforms and selling their information products or services. Today, you can show ads on Facebook to reach out to the people who are interested in your product, service or content (interest-based marketing) and can invite them to your page to build your community or tribe (like-minded people). Give value to them through your content. Conduct the introductory workshop/webinar periodically and sell your product or services to your tribe. This is called attraction-based marketing, and the mode of communication is called one-to-many through such workshops/webinars. But you have to know the niche before you build any such business, and let's discuss it below.

How to Select Your Niche?

When starting out your business have a buffet approach for your niche. Don't just rely on one niche. When you are going up just pick the three niches that sound good for you. Among that pick the one that you like the most. You can again try a few more niches before going all in one niche. The benefit of picking one niche is enormous. It will help you to eventually isolate yourself in the marketplace.

Types of Business Owners

1) Generalists

2) Specialists

Generalists: Generalists can do anything for anybody. They help a multitude of niches and do a bunch of different services.

Specialists: Specialists can do one thing for a specific type of people. They focus on one thing and one or two key revenue-driven services. The specialists also compound their knowledge and experiences by helping a specific business which in turn helps them to reach a level of mastery that generalists could never touch. Become a specialist by dominating in one niche. If necessary, stream down to micro-niche and dominate in it.

How to Dominate in your Micro Niche on Social Media

Expressing your passion on social media platforms helps you to build your personal brand. You are like a celebrity in your micro-niche here. Write a post for your audiences or create video content around your niche and post it regularly on various social media platforms.

It has been observed, that internet traffic has been moving to video content over the past few years. Creating and publishing 1, 2, 5 and 10 minutes long videos (people prefer to watch shorter videos on social media) on these platforms will help you in both ways to earn money and earn the rights (ETR) in your micro-niche. This will also be a way to generate more leads for you. Build your follower base and leverage social media in your favour. Dominate in your niche or micro-niche by using social media as a tool.

In the next chapter, we will discuss the important traits of millionaires.

16

Know the Winning Traits of Millionaires

****

"I never lose. Either I win or I learn".

-Andrew Davis

As we have seen above, running a successful business is not only limited to managing and making money out of it, but it also involves demolishing your limiting beliefs and working on your data, connections, and ideas triangle. In addition to it, you need to develop the following six traits to make your business sustainable.

1. Take a break from routine to detoxify your mind
2. Never stop learning
3. Master the art of skillful communication

4. Add value to people's lives
5. Take massive actions.
6. Tap the money leakages

You need to preserve all these six traits and in return, it will help you to maintain your millionaire status for life. They are like six spokes and you need to balance them. Let's discuss it one by one.

Figure 8. Six Spokes to Maintain Millionaire Status

Detoxify Your Mind

People detoxify their body but there are very few who detoxify their mind. The best way to detoxify your mind is to go for Vipassana every year for 10 days. Vipassana is the Pali word and literally translates into 'special seeing'. It helps you to calm your mind and be precise with reality. The idea is that you need to ground yourself with the truth of life and Vipassana is the best technique to do it. It cut off you from the chaos of the outer world and interrupts your old thinking

patterns and helps you to see the world through a new perspective. In Vipassana, you reset your mind with 10 days of silent meditation. Some of the well-known personalities who practice Vipassana are Jack Dorsey (Former CEO of Twitter), Yuval Noah Harari (Author of the book Sapiens).

Never Stop Learning

Maintain your optimum place in the industry by continuously educating yourself. Most successful people see every opportunity to train and educate themselves. They know that their income, wealth, health, and future are dependent upon their ability to continue to seek out new education (information). They read a lot of books and attend workshops or conferences related to their industry which helps them to see the bigger picture of their life or field. They connect with new people and learn new things from them. They invest a lot of time and money in self-development. They never stop learning.

Master the Art of Communication

Learn the art of speaking effectively. Remember, it takes 600 hours to prepare a one-hour effective keynote speech. Every word is strategically placed. That is the secret of the master communicator. Use this secret in business communication.

Add Value to People's Lives

Hardly anyone will tell you this secret of real wealth. We follow certain norms set by the outside world and rarely

want to peep outside it. This is applicable to wealth as well. I noticed very late in my life that I was chasing the wrong money in the form of bank deposits, mutual funds, shares, real estate, etc. This is just a money exchange. But the real wealth lies in the value exchange. Dedicate your life to the thing which can solve the world's problem or add value to people's lives. It will compensate you in a much bigger and fastest way. It will dwarf all sorts of wealth. Think about what value you can add to people's lives. It may be an app, book, or entertainment through a piece of music, dance, or singing. It would be your domain with your right on it.

Take Massive Actions

All the great people leverage their time and efforts on some concrete idea and take massive action to materialize it. At the same time, they also withstand massive risks and pressure. However, this attitude helps them to opens up a broader perspective of their lives and takes them beyond the thinking of ordinary men. Take the example of Elon Musk who does the impossible on top of the impossible. He is the supermassive action taker. He is shaping our future world through the companies like SpaceX and Tesla.

Tap the Money Leakages

According to the book, The Millionaire Next Door (Written by Thomas J. Stanley), many millionaires are frugal in nature and they save money and resources wherever they can. But that doesn't mean you'll stay in cheap hotels and save money in small bargaining. It's a scarcity mindset.

Millionaire keeps an eye on money leakages. The common man loses money every day by ignoring money leakages in various forms. Then how do they manage money? It's simple, millionaires manage money by noting down their daily expenses and tap money leakages in both business and personal life. They list down things before they go for the purchase (shopping) or budget for things in advance. This helps them to prioritise things and controls their buying behaviour. If you didn't list the things or budget it, then you may end up buying unnecessary things and will lose money. Thus, effective use of resources is one of the traits of millionaires and it is evident in their behaviour everywhere.

In the next two chapters, we will examine the social system and will also make you cautious about it.

17

School Education System

"Good teachers are more of giving right questions than giving of right answers".

-Josef Albers

Our existing education system is a copy of industrial setup like dress code, hair/nail cut, assembly, etc. (factory worker setup) and it still counts the marks in number (just like large production figure of the industrial era) rather than a skill.

It moulds every student in the same readymade curriculum package and teaches them failure is bad, cooperation is cheating, and discourages self-preparation. But all these things are part of an entrepreneur's life. Entrepreneurs know that

they have to undergo many failures before they see the final product or any success. They need cooperation to build the team and learn from each other. Self-preparation is needed to go into the depth of the problem or to tackle it from the inside. But the school system teaches exactly the opposite of the entrepreneurial spirit. Let's scrutinize the education system and the teachers by using the jackfruit story below.

Jackfruit Story

A group of forage hunter-gatherers is passing through the jungle, and they found a strange tree bearing strange fruits on it. They are not sure whether the fruit is edible or poisonous, but they have to evaluate it to overcome their hunger problem. Jack, the leader of the band, decided to try the fruit first. He ate it and found the pulp of this fruit sweet and very tasty. The other members of the group followed his example and tasted this new variety of fruit. They were very happy, as they had overcome the hunger problem and they decided to name this new fruit 'Jackfruit' in the honor of the group leader Jack. Jackfruit has become a common fruit for this group now.

In another scenario, another group of forage hunter-gatherers is passing through the jungle, and for the first time in their lives, they saw a Jackfruit tree. However, there is an old man standing below the tree and shared the details of it and its fruit like its name, texture, taste, etc., and offered them to eat this new variety of fruit. The whole group accepted the offer and they ate it. After finishing the fruit party, they moved on to the next jungle.

Now tell us which group members will remember the

details of fruits and plants for a long time. Obviously, group number one as they had overcome the hunger problem by themselves and had also christened the fruit. They will not forget its shape, size, smell, textures, etc. They can recognize this fruit anywhere in the jungle. However, the second group, on the other hand, had the information about that fruit readily available to them through an old man. Next time, even though they are passing under a jackfruit tree in another jungle, but they will not recognize it as they had hardly any association with the tree or fruit.

In the above example, the man standing under the jackfruit tree is like a teacher who is using old teaching methods and feeding information to students and they can hardly associate with it. It fails the purpose of education.

Whereas group number one is a hungry and courageous tribe, who are ready to take any risk to solve their hunger problem. This is the most important trait to survive for a long term in the jungle of entrepreneurship where you may find a fruit that is unknown to the world and you'll be the person first to taste it.

Remember here, we are living a scripted life designed by somebody else. The script is written by your parents, schools, teachers, government or big business houses. We work by default or as per norms set by our surroundings. Escape from this default life template where you have been scripted as a willful servitude and replace it with self-endorse work for unlimited growth and success.

Now let's move to the social literacy chapter of this book.

18

Impact of Government Policy on an Individual

****

"Sometimes it's not about who has more talent. It's about who's hungrier".

-Unknown

Let us understand the effect of government policy on an individual's life in this section of the book.

Housing

I have spent 30 years of my life in a Mumbai slum. There used to be queues at the community toilets. Although a toilet is fundamental in most of the countries in the world, but the rapidly growing urban India is still ignorant about it.

Slums are proliferating and most footpaths are occupied by hawkers.

There is no open space. Even mangroves and most open plots reserved for gardens and forests are occupied by the landlord mafia. When I first time moved from a slum to a rented apartment in Mumbai, I was paying half of my salary as rent. How can people with meager incomes afford to live in decent homes? This is the reason that many poor people are forced to live in unhygienic slums with minimal resources.

However, there is a solution to solve the housing problem of Mumbai and that lies in the slum itself. As per Slum Rehabilitation Authority (SRA), 48.3% of Mumbai's population lives in slums. After the redevelopment of slums, it will be possible to build a large number of houses on the remaining plot which can be rented out. The government should run rental housing schemes for the weaker section in cities like Mumbai. It will also be quick and affordable to implement. Building and selling houses to the weaker section through the lottery system has failed to provide houses to all.

I have studied the Sangharsh Nagar area in Chandivali, Mumbai, India where the government has recently built abundant houses for slum dwellers. This resulted in bringing down the rental rate in this area and helped one to live in a decent one-room-kitchen house with a toilet facility in it that is much better than in slums. This model should be implemented in all metro cities in India.

Banking Sector

Prior to 1969, it was believed that non-nationalisation of

the banking sector was the major root cause of poverty in India. This forced the government of India to reform the banking sector and nationalise all the major banks. After these reforms, the government and the people of India thought that they will succeed in eradicating poverty, but it did not benefit the common man. In 1990, India was on the verge of bankruptcy due to its failure to reform the licensing system (License Raj) and old policies.

License Raj

During the License Raj, a handful of people controlled the market. The market depended on quotas and licenses assigned to a specific product. In a conversation with one of the factory employees of the 1980s, he told me that his employer had a quota for importing certain raw materials which he was getting at a subsidised rate because of the license he had. However, he was selling it in the black market at inflated rates to those who did not have the license to import it. But the cost was ultimately borne by the end-users.

This was generating more poverty as black marketers were affecting the economy. People born after independence and up to 1990 have been affected by the licensing system. A handful of people were millionaires during this period. But in 1991, the Indian Government opened the door to liberalisation. The post-liberalisation period has created more millionaires. By the 2000s, this reform has helped many young people to overcome poverty.

The story of Asha: an evolved Generation of Mumbai after the liberalisation period

Asha, a lady I have known to her since my childhood. Coincidently, the meaning of Asha in Hindi is hope. She married a boy from a village about thirty years ago. Due to poverty, she shifted her family base from her village to Mumbai.

Since then, she has been working as a housemaid in Mumbai and her husband as a daily wage worker. She has four children. In our old locality, she was living in a 10 x 10 square foot home. It was ground plus one home structure. She leased out her upper floor to get some extra money to run her household. Even with such a minimal living, she had dreams of a better life and education for her children.

She invited me for tea a few years back. I observed the drastic changes in her life. A flat has been allotted to her after the redevelopment of our old area. Her eldest daughter is now working as a pathologist in a reputed hospital in Mumbai. The second daughter works in the animation Industry. Her son works as a site supervisor in a reputed construction company. The youngest daughter is studying in college.

Her financial situation and standard of living have completely changed. Today, she owns a well-furnished home with an extra bedroom. She is slowly but surely getting richer every day. After liberalisation, she has made her fortune in Mumbai.

I have given you a glimpse of social literacy in this chapter. It is a part of our lives because we make many decisions based on our social surroundings and that's beyond the business. But knowing this helps us to run the business for the long

term. Keep an eye on government policies and its impacts on a person's life. We have seen above how government reforms such as nationalisation of the banking sector, licensing regime, and liberalisation have affected the lives of millions of people in India. It may be different in the present time. Think about it.

19

Conclusion

****

"I'd rather live in regret of failure than in never trying".
-MJ Demarco

We are at the dawn of the knowledge zenith era where core expertise is highly valued and prioritized. In this era, your ideas make money for you. It doesn't take a lifetime to make a fortune because a person of this era can earn the wealth of life in a few weeks or months if she aligns the ideas (based on expertise) with the right data and connections.

Business around the triangle of data, connections, and ideas is a real insight. The author has implemented it himself. A simple product based on a book has been helping him to earn a fortune. Here, the book is an idea aligned with the

right data and connection angles. I am sure that this triangle will help you to decode your own business.

Use the insight of this book for limitless growth. But remember before building the business, work on your mindset and use the various tools suggested in this book. Before we conclude this book, let's assess the pros and cons of the business below:

Pros of business:

1. You acquire more clients over a period of time and enjoy the goodwill.
2. You enjoy your work most of the time as your work is based on your decisions and ideas.
3. You try to connect with the right people and want to be in the right marketplace.
4. You always look for expansion.

Cons of business:

1. A lot of things are at stake.
2. One wrong decision can ruin your business.
3. The rate of failure is very high.
4. Your market may change over a period of time; be ready for change.

It is your decision or gut feeling that will help you to choose the right path. A book like this can be a guidepost for you. I never thought of writing books in English in my life. My friends used to laugh at my broken English and unpolished pronunciation. My English was not so good because of my background. But I overcame that and became proficient in this language. I created my business framework and have written three books so far by using this language. I believe that you can achieve anything by using the insights of this book.

My father was born in 1946, just one year before India's Independence. It was an era of limited resources, but unlimited dreams for any family in India. He migrated to the city of dreams, Bombay, to make it big, but left this world halfway, not knowing how to do and take things to the next level. He worked hard as a labourer and then as a truck driver.

Living in a slum, I saw many children who weren't aware of how to work on careers. No one had guided them on how to choose a career path or create opportunities or be successful. Two of my friends died in the prime of their youth because of stepping on the wrong path. One of them has already been featured in the chapter "Change the limiting surrounding" of this book. I have survived that slum life.

Spread the success formula and let everyone know it. Leave your footprint on this planet and let's make it a better place to live.

Continue learning by subscribing to my weekly newsletter *Tools for Life* from the link given below. In this newsletter, every week I share various life tools like books, life-changing concepts, and laws of life that may help you create the best version of you.

https://manojsonawane.com/newsletter/

20

Feedback

Feel free to give me feedback on this book on my email ID-contact@manojsonawane.com. I will love to hear from you.

Manoj Sonawane

https://manojsonawane.com/
https://www.facebook.com/manojsonawane.author
https://www.instagram.com/manojasonawane/
https://www.linkedin.com/in/sonawanemanoj/

21

References

Allen, David (2001). *Getting Things Done: The Art of Stress-free Productivity*. London, UK: Piatkus.

Assaraf, John (2008). *The Answer: Grow Any Business, Achieve Financial Freedom, and Live an Extraordinary Life*. New York, USA: Crown Business. Atria Books.

Burk, Hedges (1999). *Read & Grow Rich: How the Hidden Power of Reading Can Make You Richer in All Areas of Your*. USA: I N T I Pub & Resource Books Inc.

Canfield, Jack (2013). *The Power of Focus*. UK: Simon & Schuster.

Cardone, Grant (2011). *The 10X Rule: The Only Difference Between Success*. USA: Wiley.

Collins, Jim (2005). *Built To Last: Successful Habits of Visionary Companies*. London, UK: Randon House Business Books.

DeMarco, MJ (2017). *Unscripted: Life, Liberty, and the Pursuit of Entrepreneurship.* USA: MJ DeMarco.

Dweck, Carol (2006). *Mindset: The New Psychology of Success.* New York, USA: Robinson.

Fried, Jason (2010). *Rework: Change the Way You Work Forever.*UK: Vermilion.

Gladwell, Malcolm (2008). *The Outliers: The Story of Success.* New York, USA: Hachette Book Group.

Harari, Yuval Noah (2017). *Homo Deus: A Brief History of Tomorrow.* London, UK: Penguin Random House.

Kiyosaki, Robert (1999). *Rich Dad's Cashflow quadrant: Guide to Financial Freedom.* New York, USA: Warner Books.

Koch, Richard (2008). *The 80/20 Principle: The Secret to Achieving More with Less.* New York, USA: Crown Business.

Moraes, Frank (1976). *Witness To an Era: India 1920 to the Present Day.* Delhi: Vikas Publishing House Pvt Ltd.

Robbins, Tony (2017). *Unshakable.* New York, USA: Simon & Schuster.

Sonawane, Manoj (2019). *Learning 2.0: An Inside Story on Teaching.* New Delhi, India: Penman Books.

Vance, Ashlee (2015). *Elon Musk: How the Billionaire CEO of SpaceX and Tesla is Shaping our Future.* USA: Ecco.

22

Other Books Published by Author

Preview of the book "Learning 2.0: An Inside Story on Teaching"

The book *Learning 2.0: An Inside Story on Teaching* has reached the #1 Amazon Bestseller spot out of the top 100 books under the category of Educational Philosophy.

What you'll get from the book:

1. How to connect with students (or children) using stories (1-minute stories).
2. How to create new content (stories) and use them in learning and teaching methods.
3. Learning Psychology- how to remove the fear of any subject by using NLP (Neuro-Linguistic Programming).
4. Accelerated learning which involves students through self-learning process where teachers (or parents) have to act as mediators and let the students learn and act.

All four parts are based on contemporary methods implemented in the education field recent times.

This book has been featured in the *Free Press Journal newspaper* and received the following review:

"Learning 2.0' by Manoj Sonawane could well be considered an informative dossier for all those who want to acquire knowledge as well as pass it on to others, the book has a much wider reach and implications, beyond teacher-pupil domain".

Get your Paperback or Kindle copy of this book from the link >>> **http://amzn.to/3igXeEs**

Preview of the book "How to Create Agile Library: Build Information Services on Cloud"

The book **"How to Create Agile Library: Build Information Services on Cloud"** has received hundreds of e-copy downloads within a week of its launch from countries like the UK, Latin America, Malaysia, Africa, etc.

In this book, we will build the 'agile library' by using various e-tools ranging from cloud storage to e-content management to online delivery of information and it would be a handy guide for you to create your online library.

The book will start with a conversation on how the IT industry shifted from the 'waterfall model' to an 'agile model' and provided benefits to the end customers.

In the next part, the book will use this 'agile model' of the IT industry to shift the traditional library services into an 'agile library' and while doing it, it will also apply various e-tools or resources to build the information services on the cloud and make the library truly agile.

In addition to the above following would be your take-aways from this book.

1) How to get 200 GB of cloud space free for your information services.

2) How to use Facebook as a social learning platform for your library.

3) How to Market Library Information products and Services by using emails.

4) How to rethink Library as a creative space and mould it as per the market demand.

Get your Paperback or Kindle copy of this book from the link >>> **https://amzn.to/3qVlpwN**